# THIRTY-ONE HYMNS
# TO
# THE STAR GODDESS
## Frater Achad

**Kessinger Publishing's Rare Reprints
Thousands of Scarce and Hard-to-Find Books!**

We kindly invite you to view our extensive catalog list at:
http://www.kessinger.net

# THIRTY-ONE HYMNS
# TO
# THE STAR GODDESS
## Frater Achad

Sure Fire
Press

# XXXI HYMNS

# TO THE STAR GODDESS

*Who is Not*

BY XIII : *which is* ACHAD

CHICAGO
WILL RANSOM
MCMXXIII

# TABLE OF CONTENTS

| | | |
|---|---|---|
| I | *Invocation* | 7 |
| II | *The Brook* | 8 |
| III | *The Rose Garden* | 9 |
| IV | *The Fox Glove* | 10 |
| V | *The Storm* | 11 |
| VI | *The Hole in the Roof* | 12 |
| VII | *The Design* | 13 |
| VIII | *The Snow Drift* | 14 |
| IX | *Daylight* | 15 |
| X | *The Bird* | 16 |
| XI | *The Moral* | 17 |
| XII | *The Invisible Foot Prints* | 18 |
| XIII | *The Finger Tips* | 19 |
| XIV | *The Well of Stars* | 20 |
| XV | *The Icicles of Isis* | 21 |
| XVI | *Purple Mist* | 22 |
| XVII | *The Infinite Within* | 23 |
| XVIII | *The Rainbow* | 24 |
| XIX | *Dropped Dew* | 25 |

| | | |
|---|---|---:|
| XX | *Twilight* | 26 |
| XXI | *The Dog Star* | 27 |
| XXII | *Pot-pouri* | 28 |
| XXIII | *Red Swansdown* | 30 |
| XXIV | *Passing Clouds* | 31 |
| XXV | *The Coiled Serpent* | 32 |
| XXVI | *Love and Unity* | 33 |
| XXVII | *The Riddle* | 34 |
| XXVIII | *Sayings* | 35 |
| XXIX | *The Falling Star* | 36 |
| XXX | *Justice* | 37 |
| XXXI | *Not* | 38 |

*The quotations attributed to the Star Goddess in this volume are from Liber Al vel Legis Sub Figura* CCXX *as delivered by* LXXVIII *unto* DCLXVI

I ∴ *Invocation*

MOTHER of the Sun, Whose Body is White with the Milk of the Stars, bend upon Thy servant and impart unto him Thy Secret Kiss!

Enkindle within him the Holy Ecstasy Thou hast promised unto them that love Thee; the Ecstasy which redeemeth from all pain.

Hast Thou not proclaimed: All the sorrows are but shadows, they pass and are done, but there is that which remains? That the Universe is Pure Joy—that Thou givest unimaginable Joys on Earth—that Thou demandest naught in sacrifice?

Let me then rejoice, for therein may I serve Thee most fully. Let it be Thy Joy to see my joy; even as Thou hast promised in Thy Holy Book!

Now, therefore, am I Joyful in Thy Love.

AUMN

## II ∴ The Brook

I WANDERED beside the running stream, and mine eyes caught the glint of Thy Starry Orbs in the swirling waters.

So is it with my mind; it flows on towards the Great Sea of Understanding wherein I may come to know Thee more fully.

Sometimes, as it journeys, it threatens to overflow its banks in its eagerness to reflect a wider image of Thine Infinite Body.

Ah! How the very stones, over which flow the life of my being, thrill at the tender caress of Thy reflected Image.

Thou, too, art Matter; it is I — Thy Complement — who am Motion! Therefore these very stones are of Thee, but the Spirit — the Life — is the very Self of me; mine Inmost Being.

Flow on, O Stream! Flow on, O Life! Towards the Great Sea of Understanding, the Great Mother.

## III ∴ The Rose Garden

LONG have I lain and waited for Thee in the Rose Garden of Life; yet ever Thou withholdest Thyself from mine Understanding.

As I lay I contemplated Thy nature as that of an Infinite Rose.

Petals, petals, petals . . . but where, O Beauteous One, is Thy Heart?

Hast Thou no Heart? Are Thy petals Infinite so that I may never reach the Core of Thy Being?

Yet, Thou hast said: "I love you! I yearn to you! Pale or purple, veiled or voluptuous, I who am all pleasure and purple, and drunkenness of the innermost sense, desire you: Come unto me!"

Yea! Mine innermost sense is drunken; it is intoxicated upon the Dew of the Rose. Thy Heart is my Heart; there is no difference, O Beloved.

When I shall have penetrated to the Heart of Thine Infinite Rose, there shall I find Myself.

But I shall never come to myself—only to Thee.

## IV ∴ The Fox Glove

TALL and straight as a Fox Glove do I stand before Thee, Mother of Heaven.

The flower of my being is given over to a strange conceit; I grow up towards the Stars and not towards the Sun.

Art Thou not Mother of the Sun?

Thus have I blasphemed the Lord and Giver of Life for Thy sake. Yet am I not ashamed, for in forgetting the Sun I am become the Sun — Thy Son — yet a thousand times more Thy Lover.

The foxes have holes and the birds of the air have nests, but now I have nowhere to lay my head; for tall and straight as a Fox Glove do I stand before Thee. My resting place is the Womb of the Stars.

Yet all that I may comprehend of Thine Infinite Body is but as the Glove upon one of Thy soft sweet hands, touching the Earth, not hurting the little flowers.

## v ∴ The Storm

A DARK NIGHT and the Storm. The lightning flashes between Thee and me. I am dazzled so that I see Thee not.

So in the depths of my being flash the fires of life; they blind me to the Understanding of Thee and Thine Infinite Body of Stars.

Yet I see Thee reflected in the body of her I love, as we lie with quivering limbs awaiting the coming of the sound of thunder.

She fears the thunder, and turns within herself for consolation.

But even there the Lightning flameth, for I have loosed the fires of my being within the dark recess — in honour of the Storm and of Thine Infinite Body which I see not.

## VI ∴ The Hole in The Roof

ONCE I knew an ancient serpent. He delighted to bask in the Sunshine which penetrated through a tiny hole in the roof of the cave.

He was old and very wise.

He said: "Upon me is concentrated the Light of the whole Universe."

But a little brown beetle, who had long lived in the cave with him, looked up, and spreading his wings passed out through the hole in the roof—into the Infinite Beyond.

Thus, forsaking wisdom, would I come to Thee, Beloved Lady of the Starry Heavens.

## VII ∴ The Design

STRANGE CURVES: and every Curve a Number woven into a Musical and Harmonious Pattern.

Such was the design showed me by my friend when first we met.

It was like an exchange of greetings by means of an inward recognition.

Oh! Could I but grasp the Ever-changing Design of Thy Star Body, Mother of Heaven!

Yet, it is written: "Every man and every woman is a star. Every number is infinite; there is no difference."

Such then is Life, for those who love Thee: Strange Curves, and every Curve a Number woven into a Musical and Harmonious Design.

## VIII ∴ The Snow Drift

MY body was blue as Thine, O Beloved, when they found me. I was stiff as if held in a close embrace. Nor was I conscious of aught but Thee, till the small fires of Earth brought me back with an agony of tingling pain.

How came I to be lost in the snow-drift?

I remember how I had taken shelter from the blinding storm. The snow fell about me, and I waited, turning my thought to Thee.

Then did I realize how every snow-flake is built as a tiny star. I looked closer, burying my face in the white pile, as in Thy Bosom. Mine arms embraced the snow-drift; I clung to it in a mad ecstasy.

Thus would I have pressed Thy Body to mine, wert Thou not Infinite and I but as tiny as a star-flake.

So was my body frozen—as by the utmost cold of inter-stellar space.

It was blue as Thine when they found me locked in Thine embrace.

## IX ∴ Daylight

IN the Daylight I see not Thy Body of Stars, O Beloved.

The little light of the Sun veils the Great Light of the Stars, for to-day Thou seemest distant.

The Sun burns like a great Torch, and Earth seems as one of His little Spheres, filled with life.

I am but a tiny spermatozoon, but within me is the fiery and concentrated essence of Life.

Draw me up into Thyself, O Sun! Project me into the Body of Our Lady Nuit!

Thus shall a new Star be born, and I shall see Thee even in the Daylight, O Beloved.

# x ∴ The Bird

ONCE I bought a little bird; his cage was very small; it had only one perch. He was so young he had not even learned to sing, but he chirped gladly when I brought him home.

Then I raised the bars of his cage, and without a moment's hesitation he flew out into the room, and spying the cage of the love-birds, perched upon it and examined it carefully.

Not long afterwards another and stronger cage was obtained for the love-birds, for they had pecked through some of the frail bars. When the little bird was offered the discarded cage, he quickly hopped from his tiny one to theirs.

Now he has three perches and room for his tail, and when we open the door of his cage he refuses to come out. Perhaps he fears to lose what he had once coveted and then obtained.

Herein lies the secret of Government. Give the people what will make them reasonably comfortable; let them have three perches and room for their tails; and forgetting their slavery and restrictions, they will be content.

Hast Thou not said "The slaves shall serve," Lady of the Starry Heaven?

# XI ∴ The Moral

THERE is another moral to the story of the little bird. Having gained his desire for a larger cage, he forgot his true longing for Freedom.

The door remained open; the room was before him, wherein he could stretch his wings and fly.

Yet he preferred his cage.

The wide world might have been his had he known how to use it, but he was not ready for that; he would have perished of cold had I let him out into the wintry snow.

Let those who would travel the Mystic Path remember this: Earth Consciousness is an illusion and a limitation. When it frets us, like a little cage, our chance for greater freedom comes.

But when a larger cage is offered us—when we obtain *Dhyana*—let us not rest there thinking ourselves free. The door is open, *Samadhi* lies beyond, and beyond that, when we are ready for it, the Real Freedom, *Nirvana*.

O Lady of the Stars, let me not be content till I penetrate the ultimate bars and am Free—One with the Infinitely Great as with the Infinitely Small.

## XII ∴ The Invisible Foot Prints

LONG have I roamed the Earth delighting in the Good, the Beautiful and the True; ever seeking the spots where these seem to be most Perfect.

There is joy in this wandering among the flowers of life, but Thy Joy, O Beloved, is to be desired above all.

Now I seek a resting place, I am set upon a new Quest, to Worship at Thy feet.

For it is written of Thee: "Bending down, a lambent flame of blue, all touching, all penetrant, her lovely hands upon the black earth, and her lithe body arched for love, and her soft feet not hurting the little flowers.

Oh! That I might discover Thine Invisible Footprints upon the Earth and there come to the Understanding of Thy Being, O Beloved.

## XIII ∴ The Finger Tips

OR, it may be, O Beloved, I shall discover the imprints of Thy finger tips amid the flowers or upon the Black Earth.

Hath not Nemo a Garden that he tendeth? Doth he not also labour in the Black Earth?

Who knoweth when Thy hands may grasp me and draw me up into Thine arms, there to nestle at Thy breast, to feed upon the Milk of the Stars?

Beloved, verily this tending of the Garden of the World—although the labor may seem heavy—leadeth to a Great Reward. As Thou hast said: "Certainty, not faith, while in life upon death, rest, ecstasy." Nor dost Thou demand aught in sacrifice.

What do the Bhaktis know of Love? They see the Beloved everywhere.

But when I am one with Thee, O Beloved, I shall not see Thee, for I shall know Thee as Thou art.

## XIV ∴ The Well of Stars

I KNOW a hidden well of clearest water. Naught but the coping of delicate pink onyx is visible until the secret spring be touched.

Then beware! For above the entrance hangs a fiery sword.

Few find this Well or know its Secret; there are but two roads leading thereto.

From the broad Mountain summit we may search the slopes for a vision of the Woodland Delta where grow the Trees of Eternity, or we may journey through the Valley between the Ivory Hills—if we fear not the purple shadows and the black pit-fall.

From Thee we came; to Thee may we return, O Well of Living Stars!

## XV ∴ The Icicles of Isis

IT hath been written how the Old King dreamed of his banished peacock, entombed in a palace of ice, who cried: "The Icicles of Isis are falling on my head."

Thus it is with those who are banished to the Palace of the Moon—for the Word of Sin is Restriction.

Oh! Lady of the Starry Heavens, let me not become frozen at the touch of the cold Veil of Isis. For the Moon is but the dead reflector of the Sun, and He but the youngest of Thy Children of Light.

Let me lift Thy Peacock Veil of a Million Starry Eyes, O Beloved!

Show Thy Star Splendour, O Nuit; bid me within Thine house to dwell!

# XVI ∴ Purple Mist

THE delicate purple mist steams up from the hills: I watch and wait for the meaning of it all.

Sometimes it seems like the incense smoke of Aspiration ascending towards the Sun—giver of Light, Life, Love and Liberty to the Children of Earth.

But the Sun is going down behind the Mountains, and Thy Starry Lamps glow in the Sky.

Is not the Lamp above the Altar a symbol of the Desire of the Higher to draw up the lower to Itself?

So, O Lady of Heaven, I liken the Mist to the life-breath of Souls who pant for Thee here below.

And I remember Thy words:

> *Above, the gemmèd azure is*
>    *The naked splendour of Nuit;*
> *She bends in ecstacy to kiss*
>    *The secret ardours of Hadit.*
> *The wingèd globe, the starry blue,*
> *Are mine, O Ankh-af-na-khonsu!*

I, too, would ascend as a delicate purple mist that steams up from the Hills. Art Thou not all Pleasure and Purple?

## XVII ∴ *The Infinite Within*

I WOULD that I were as the feminine counterpart of Thee, O Beloved; then would I draw the Infinite within.

Yet since Thy Pure Being must ever be more refined than this body of mine I should interpenetrate every part of Thee with my living flesh.

Thus, O Beloved, should we enter into a new and more complete embrace: not as of earth wherein the male uniteth with the female by means of the physical organs of love, but with every atom of my being close pressed to every atom of Thine—within and without.

Then, O Beloved, would I cry unto the Lord of the Primum Mobile to teach me the Art of the Whirling Motion of Eternity.

Thus, whirling within Thee, our never-ending nuptial feast shall be celebrated, and a new System of Revolving Orbs be brought to birth.

Ah! the shrill cry of Ecstacy of that Refined Rapture—the Orgasm of the Infinite Within.

## XVIII ∴ The Rainbow

As I sat in the shelter of the forest glade, my eye caught the multi-coloured gleam of diamonds. I looked again; the Sun rays were playing upon the dew which clung to a little curved twig.

It seemed like a tiny rainbow of promise.

Then, while I watched in wonder, a small grey spider bridged the arch of the bow with his silken thread.

Ah! My Beloved, thus, too, hath the Spider of Destiny woven his silken rope from extreme to extreme of the Great Rainbow of Promise.

Fate hath fitted me as an Arrow to the String of Destiny in the bow of the Sun.

But Whose Hand shall draw that Mighty Bow, O Beloved, and send me upon fleet wings to my resting place within Thine Heart?

## XIX ∴ Dropped Dew

As I came from tending the Rose Garden and was about to return to my humble shelter, my eyes caught the gleam of dropped dew like a tiny trail along the path.

It was very early; the Sun had not yet re-arisen; the Stars still twinkled faintly in the sky.

Who could have come before me to the Garden?

I followed the trail of dew, stooping down so that I saw in each crystal drop the reflection of a tiny star.

Thus came I to my lady's chamber; she it was who carrying roses had left this silvery thread as a clue to her hiding place.

When I found her, her eyes were closed, as she pressed the fragrant pink blossoms to her white breast.

Then did I bury my face in the blossoms, and I saw not her eyes when she opened them in wonder.

Thus, too, would I follow the Star-trail of Dropped Dew, ere the re-arisen Sun hides Thee from me, O My Beloved!

Thus would I come to Thee and bury my face in Thy Breast amid the Roses of Heaven.

Nor should I dare to look into Thine eyes, having discovered Thy secret — the Dew of Love — the Elixir of Life.

# XX ∴ Twilight

TWILIGHT . . . and in a few brief moments the Stars will begin to peep. I will await Thee, here amid the heather, O Beloved.

I wait . . . no stars appear for a mist has stolen up from the foot of the mountains.

Thus I waited for a sight of Thy Star Body till the cold damp mist of suppressed emotion chilled my being and my reason returned.

The woman stood girt with a sword before me. Emotion was overcome by clarity of perception. Then did I remember Thy words: "The Khabs is in the Khu not the Khu in the Khabs. Worship then the Khabs and behold my light shed over ye."

Thus turned I my thoughts within, so that I became concentrated upon the Khabs—the Star of mine inmost being. Then did Thy Light arise as a halo of rapture, and I came a little to lie in Thy bosom.

But I offered one particle of dust—and I lost all in that hour.

Such is the Mystery of Her who demandest naught in sacrifice.

The twilight is returned.

## XXI ∴ The Dog Star

WISDOM hath said: "Be not animal; refine thy rapture! Then canst thou bear more joy!"

I have been like an unleashed hound before Thee, O Beloved. I have striven towards Thee and Thou seest in me only the Dog Star.

Yet will I not fall into the Pit called Because, there to perish with the dogs of reason. There is no reason in me; I seek Understanding, O Mother of Heaven.

Thus, with my face buried in the black earth, do I turn my back upon Thee. I will refine my rapture.

So Thou mayest behold me as I am, and so Thou shalt Understand at last, O Beloved; for *in reverse* Thou readest this DOG aright.

Hast Thou not said: "There is none other?"

## XXII ∴ Pot-pouri

THE roses are falling. This is the night of the full moon whereon the children of Sin attend the Sacred Circle.

Therein they will sit divided—but not for love's sake—for they know Thee not—O Beloved. Into the Elements, the fiery, the watery, the airy and the earthly Signs are they divided when they gather at the Full Moon within the forest.

I wandered down the deep shadowy glade, there I espied a tiny sachet of pot-pouri, dropped—maybe—from the streaming girdle of one of the maidens.

Tenderly I raised it. Its perfume is like unto the perfume of her I love. She, too, perhaps, has heard the call of the moon and is even now on her way to the secret tryst.

But hast Thou not said: "Let there be no difference made among you between any one thing and any other thing; for thereby there cometh hurt." What matter then the name of the maiden? What matter the flowers of which it is composed?

Yet dare I not burn this incense unto Thee, O Beloved, because of Thine hair, the Trees of Eternity.

Oh! Little sachet of pot-pouri, thou hast reminded me of her I love, for the roses are falling, it is the night of the Full Moon and the children of Sin gather to attend the Sacred Circle.

## XXIII ∴ Red Swansdown

IT hath been told how Parzival shot and brought down the Swan of Ecstacy as it winged over the Mountain of the Grail.

But there is within the archives another story, unheard by the ears of men.

From the breast of the Eternal Swan floated one downy feather, steeped in blood. This did the youngest and least worthy of the Knights hide tenderly in his bosom till he concealed it within the hard pillow of his lonely couch.

Night after night that holy pillow became softer; sweeter and sweeter were his dreams. And one night — the night of the crowning of Parzival — he was granted the Great Vision wherein the Stars became like flecks of Swansdown upon the Breast of Heaven, each living and throbbing, for they were steeped in Blood.

Then did every atom of his being become a Star racing joyfully through the Great Body of the Lady of Heaven. Thus in sweet sleep came he into the Great Beyond.

Grant unto me Thy Pillow of Blood and Ecstacy, O Beloved!

## XXIV ∴ Passing Clouds

A DARK NIGHT: Not a star is visible, but presently the moon shines out through a rift in the clouds. And I remember; "The sorrows are but shadows, they pass and are done, but there is that which remains."

Yet is the moon but illusion.

A dull day: but presently the Sun is seen as the clouds are dispelled by His light.

Is He that which remains?

Night once more: the Sun is lost to sight, only the moon reminds me of His presence. The clouds scud swiftly across the Sky and disappear.

Thy Star Body is visible, O Beloved; all the sorrows and shadows have passed and *there* is *that* which remains.

When clouds gather, let me never forget Thee, O Beloved!

## XXV ∴ The Coiled Serpent

THUS have I heard:

The ostrich goeth swiftly; with ease could he outstrip those who covet his tail-feathers, yet when danger cometh he burieth his head in the sand.

The tortoise moveth slowly and when embarrassed he stoppeth, withdrawing into his own shell; yet he passeth the hare.

The hare sleepeth when he should be swiftly moving; he runneth in his dreams thinking himself at the goal.

But the Coiled Serpent hath wisdom, for he hideth his tail and it is not coveted; he raiseth his head and fears not; he moveth slowly like the tortoise, yet withdraweth not; he nestles close to the hare, darting his tongue with swiftness, yet falleth not asleep by the wayside.

Would that I had the Wisdom of the Coiled Serpent, O Beloved, for Thou hast said: "Put on the wings, arouse the coiled splendour within you: come unto me!"

## XXVI ∴ Love and Unity

TWENTY-SIX is the numeration of the Inneffable Name, but It concealeth Love and Unity.

The Four-lettered Name implieth Law, yet it may be divided for love's sake; for Love is the law.

The Four-lettered Name is that of the elements, but it may be divided for the chance of Union; for there is Unity therein.

There is but One Substance and One Love and while these be twenty-six they are One through thirteen which is but a half thereof.

Thus do I play with numbers who would rather play with One and that One Love.

For Thou hast said: "There is naught that can unite the divided but love!"

And is not Achad Ahebah?

## XXVII ∴ The Riddle

WHAT is that which cometh to a point yet goeth in a circle?

This, O Beloved, is a dark saying, but Thou hast said: "My colour is black to the blind, but blue and gold are seen of the seeing. Also I have a secret glory for them that love me."

And Hadit hath declared: "There is a veil; that veil is black."

I would that I could tear aside the veil, O Beloved, for seeing Thee as Thou art, I might see Thee everywhere, even in the darkness that cometh to a point yet goeth in a circle.

For Hadit, the core of every star, says "It is I that go," and Thou, Mother of the Stars, criest "To me! To me!"

Resolve me the Riddle of Life, O Beloved, for loving Thee I would behold Thy Secret Glory.

## XXVIII ∴ Sayings

ISIS hath said: "I am all that was and that is and that shall be, and no mortal hath lifted my veil."

Who cares what is back of the moon?

Jehovah showed his back unto Moses, saying: "No man hath seen my face at any time."

Who cares to face the elements?

Hadit hath said: "I am life and the giver of life; therefore is the knowledge of me the knowledge of death."

Who cares to know death?

But Thou, O Beloved, hath said: "I give unimaginable joys on earth, certainty, not faith, while in life upon death, peace unutterable, rest, ecstacy; nor do I demand aught in sacrifice."

Who would not long to invoke Thee under Thy Stars, O Beloved?

## XXIX .·. The Falling Star

FALLING, falling, falling! Thus fall the Rays from Thy Body of Stars upon this tiny planet, O Beloved! Innumerable streams of Light like Star-rain upon the black earth.

Since every man and woman is a star, their lives are like unto streams of light concentrated upon every point in Space.

As I lay with arms out-stretched, my bare body shining like ivory in the darkness, my scarlet abbai flung wide, mine eyes fixed upon the star-lit Heaven; I felt that I, too, was falling, falling, falling, in an ecstacy of fear and love into the void abyss of space.

Then did I remember that Thou art continuous. Beneath, above, around me art Thou. And lo, from a falling star I became as a comet wheeling in infinite Circles, each at a different angle, till my course traced out the Infinite Sphere that is the Symbol of Thee, O Beloved.

Then did I aspire to find the Centre of All.

And even now I am falling, falling, falling.

## XXX ∴ Justice

I AM a Fool, O Beloved, and therefore am I One or Nought as the fancy takes me.

Now am I come to Justice, so that I may be All or Naught according to the direction of vision.

No Breath may stir the Feather of Truth, therefore is Justice ALone in L. Yet the Ox-goad is Motion and the Breath Matter if it be called the Ox which is also A.

How foolish are these thoughts, which are but as the Sword in the hand of Justice. They are as unbalanced as the Scales that stir not, being fixed in the grasp of the figure of Law above the Court House of a great City.

But Thou hast said: "Love is the law, love under will."

And Love is the Will to Change and Change is the Will to Love.

Even in the stern outline of the Scales of Justice do I perceive the Instrument of Love, and in the Life Sentence, the Mystery of Imprisonment in Thy Being, O Beloved!

XXXI ∴ *Not*

THREE Eternities are passed . . . I have outstripped a million Stars in my race across Thy Breast—The Milky Way.

When shall I come to the Secret Centre of Thy Being?

Time, thou thief, why dost thou rob the hungry babe? Space, thou hadst almost deceived me.

O Lady Nuit, let me not confound the space-marks!

Then, O Beloved, Thy Word came unto me, as it is written: "All touching; All penetrant."

Thus left I Time and Space and Circumstance, and every Star became as an atom in my Body, when it became Thy Body. Now never shall I be known, for it is I that go.

But Thou, O Beloved, though Thou art infinitely Great, art Thou not energized by the Invisible Point—the Infinitely Small?

   A Million Eternities are Present. Deem
     not of Change; This is the
      Here and Now,
       and I am
        NOT